A Chaplain's Prison Jacket

The Duty of Serving Society's

Multi-Faith Prison Culture

A CHAPLAIN'S PRISON JACKET:
the Duty of Serving Society's
Multi-Faith Prison Culture

Author Joseph Luce
ISBN: 9798385868766
KDP Amazon, Seattle, WA

CalvaryHillPublishing
Series title "Diplomacy in specific areas
of cultural engagement"
Part of a series of books about life

© Copyright 2023 Joseph Paul Luce
All rights reserved.
Except for brief quotations in critical publications
or reviews, no part of this work may be reproduced
in any form without prior written
permission from the author.

DEDICATION

This booklet is dedicated to the men and women who serve inside the prison system as custody staff; especially those who have been seriously injured from assaults by those they watch over, and most especially those whose ultimate commitment to public safety has cost them their lives. May the God of heaven and earth provide for and sustain and care for the families of these courageous men and women.

TABLE OF CONTENTS

OPENING COMMENTS 1

DISCUSSION SEGMENTS:

ONE	The Tool Belt	5
TWO	Your Personal Spirituality	11
THREE	A Heart for Service	25
FOUIR	The Religious Calendar	33
FIVE	Simple Respect: Part One	57
SIX	Simple Respect: Part Two	61
SEVEN	Part of a Uniform?	67
EIGHT	Pen and Paper	73
NINE	Closing Reflections	77

Selected Bibliography 81

OPENING COMMENTS

It may be helpful to know that the term "jacket" historically has its own meanings in prison culture. To prison inmates and prison workers, a jacket can mean a "folder," a "past crime summary sheet;" or, most importantly, a "reputation." Your "jacket" is how you're seen. The metaphor of a chaplain's prison jacket is not a fashion statement; it is aimed at understanding the significance of the manner, bearing, and reputation of a prison chaplain in a multi-faith correctional institution.

What is a prison chaplain's reputation? The point of the illustration—the meaning of the visual metaphor of the "jacket"—is to deepen multi-faith religious literacy. The chaplain or chapel administrative assistant or religious program coordinator becomes known by their commitment to religious literacy when working around the many diverse religions inside today's prisons. You serve others who are unlike you.

This book aims to expand the potential prison religious program worker's repertoire with specific administrative tools and skills to honor this duty of prison work in today's multi-faith prison culture; a duty of religious literacy.

The booklet "A Chaplain's Prison Jacket" is intended to help prison religious program personnel respond to this specific, specialized duty to serve society by compassionately protecting religious freedoms for the different faith groups in today's multi-faith prison culture.

As one chaplain writes,

> "In prison, you're transparent. There's a grapevine. The people confined there are street-smart and cynical; there's no putting on a false persona. The inmates will compare notes on you, and any flaws or acting will come out and destroy your credibility. You have to keep it real. You have to be honest and open and have the patience of Job."[1]

Prison facility employees are known to inmates and institutional staff by their words and behavior. These words and actions reveal the chaplain's attitudes and lead to the "jacket" or reputation others will perceive.

---

[1] Earl Smith, *Death Row Chaplain: Unbelievable True Stories from America's Most Notorious Prison* (New York: Howard, 2015), 156.

Prison culture in some ways reflects the wider culture around it. Because the incarcerated in America retain their right of freedom of religious expression, the variety of religions inside a prison tends to replicate the variety and assortment of religions in culture as a whole.

The chaplain does not have to know the fullest, deepest depths of theology of all these diverse religions, but does need cultural awareness and relational understanding to gain an adequate level of practical familiarity with them. Religious literacy becomes a trademark of the duty to serve in today's multi-faith prisons.

This booklet is written for potential and new fulltime prison chaplains, not for prison ministry volunteers or contract clergy hired to serve one specific religion only. This booklet is written to help facility employees with duties over a broad multi-faith jurisdiction.

Questions at the end of each Discussion Segment provide talking points to stimulate conversations among potential or new prison facility religious program employees. These questions are suitable for anyone who may be considering, or is new to, prison facility religious program work.

"A Chaplain's Prison Jacket" is based upon a visual picture as one way to describe prison religious work. What is important is the way that a prison chaplain's outward religious demeanor and outward actions carry out the duty need in today's multi-faith religious prison context. The "jacket" is just a metaphor. It means "reputation" for reliability; it means skill in religious literacy; it means compassion care.

Chaplains, administrative chapel assistants, and religious program coordinators from all faith backgrounds can actively and humbly care for the needs of incarcerated persons of all religions, races, and backgrounds.

Highly skilled religious literacy and the commitment to serve become the outwardly-visible trademarks of the contemporary chaplain.

DISCUSSION SEGMENT ONE

The Tool Belt

In our metaphor, "A Chaplain's Prison Jacket" has many pockets. Each pocket illustrates how to carry out duty and service in today's multi-faith prison culture. Each pocket contains tools of the trade.

The metaphor of this booklet helps a new or prospective prison chaplain to understand the correctional setting and its unique practical needs in today's multi-faith prison culture.

A brief look at something simple and tangible is appropriate before looking deeper into the visual metaphor of a chaplain's prison jacket. Underneath the jacket is the all-important belt. That's right, a belt around the middle.

A prison worker's belt acts like a tradesman's tool belt. Many trades and professions utilize a tool belt to carry necessary implements or apparatus, and prison workers are no exception.

For the prison chaplain, a leather belt is a great way to carry a two-way facility radio. Does this belt have to be leather? No, of course not; it just has to be strong and reliable. Leather is strong enough to carry the radio safely and predictably, though of course some modern materials are as well.

A belt also may also carry a Universal Precautions first aid kit, so that a chaplain may help respond to a real emergency such as a fallen inmate or staff member.

These things are real, not symbolic. They are tangible realities of prison work.

Another imperative reality of the prison worker is the key set. Keys, key sets, and key control always rank highly on the list of daily priorities for the prison worker. Retired prison chaplain Peter Grant describes his key and radio checkout process:

> I come to the Control Center window. It has waist-high breeze-block walls topped with bullet-proof glass all round...Inside it all radio communications, cameras and sliding doors in the complex are monitored and controlled...There's a uniformed officer standing at the window. "Hi Tom. Key 236, radio 85 and a spare battery, please." I drop three round brass chits into the sliding door beneath the glass.... Tom nods, slides the drawer open on his side and retrieves them,

then turns to the key cupboard beside him...He takes them from the hook, hangs one of my chits on it, then walks to the back of the room where long lines of radios are plugged into their recharging docks...He brings the items back to the window, dropping them into the drawer with a clatter... "There you go, Chaplain." "Thanks, Tom." ...I turn on the radio, check the charge light, make sure the channel's properly set, all the switches are in the right positions, then clip it onto my web belt next to the key-holder. [2]

When learning to use keys and prison locks, consider the acronym "CLICK." Think of each of the letters C, L, I, C, and K being reminders about the actual importance of safety and security inside the prison setting.

> **C.** **Check** the lock. Is the door locked or unlocked? Precisely which key does the lock call for?
>
> **L.** **Look** at your key set for that matching key.
>
> **I.** **Insert** your key carefully. You do not want to bend or break a key, especially inside a lock. This would

---

[2] Peter Grant, *Walls, Wire, Bars and Souls: A Chaplain Looks At Prison Life* (San Bernardino: Fynbos, 2013), 4-5.

disable the lock and hamper response to potential emergencies.

C. **Check** the lock again. If you meant to unlock the door, have you? If the door needs to lock, have you locked it? Check the handle to ensure the door is locked. Check the door to make sure it is fully latched shut. Check the door by giving it a tug or a good shake. Check it; someone's life may depend on that later.

K. **Key** back onto key holder. Listen for the click. A consistent habit of returning the key to your key holder is essential, as is a habit of checking to ensure the key holder has not stuck open.

In prisons it is mandatory to quickly develop a second nature with safety and security patterns for keys, locks, and doors.

Just remember, **C. L. I. C. K**.: Check the lock, Look at your key set, Insert carefully, Check the door/lock again, Key back onto key holder with a **CLICK!**

Keys and loud slamming doors are a reminder of the realities of the prison world. Doors and locks keep people safe.

At the end of each work day, a pattern of checking your key holder to make sure it is empty saves you a long trip back to the prison after what should have been the end of your work shift.

And remember: Never take your keys out of the prison.

Never.

Discussion Segment One Questions

1. Get to know your classmates. How new are you to the field of corrections? How familiar are you with institutional religious program operations, and where did you learn about them?
2. What kinds of things do you feel you need to gain greater familiarity with, in order to help you do this type of work?
3. Have you used a tool belt or tool apron in a previous job? Describe the advantages of using a tool belt in that context.

4. Describe a time when you and someone else used cell phones, walkie talkies, or two way radios. What were some of the benefits of reliable two-way communication at that time?
5. What might be some consequences in a prison setting if you were unable to communicate your location and situation to others?
6. Have you ever lost a key, or set of keys? What were the lost keys originally for? What concerns did you have about these lost keys being found and misused? Identify some ways this could apply to the prison setting, such as the need for notification in the event of lost items.
7. Talk about how misplaced items such as cell phones or wallets might seem harmless outside the prison but may create security situations when found by inmates.

DISCUSSION SEGMENT TWO
Your Personal Spirituality

Now that the tangible, actual tool belt has been explored, it is time to look more closely into the visual metaphor of a chaplain's prison jacket. Lightly patting the jacket, the hand finds that something is inside the inner right pocket. What is it?

Imagine this pocket holding the Holy Scripture or sacred writings of the chaplain's own personally-held religious beliefs and faith.

The duty to serve society by serving as a prison religious program worker requires serving the needs of inmates from faith groups who are different from and dissimilar from one's own. Does this mean to water down one's own beliefs? Absolutely not.

In fact maintaining a pure adherence to one's faith is a vital survival tool in the prison setting. At the same time, arrogant or haughty self-righteousness is never spiritually good. We always believe what we believe, but cannot force our beliefs while serving in this line of work.

Because incarcerated persons do not lose their right to freedom of religious expression, a prison religious program employee today needs to care for the needs of persons of diverse religions in order to be effective. You are not expected to stop believing your faith or creed. You must, however, provide for the needs of people of diverse religions.

For a prison religious worker – whether the chaplain or the chapel administrative assistant – this may create an inner tension of religious conviction.

Keep in mind you serve persons from perhaps fifteen to twenty religions or faith traditions other than your own. The religious program staff does well to work through this inner tension carefully and thoroughly, ideally with a more seasoned mentor or persons from their own faith outside the prisons, such as their endorser.

Again, you are not being asked to set aside your religious beliefs and background, only to protect others' rights to express their own religious beliefs.

At the forefront of today's pluralistic culture is the reality that whatever your favorite Holy Scripture or sacred writings might be, your duty as facility chaplain or administrative assistant or religious program coordinator or religious services provider remains: to provide well for the needs of others, including those who believe differently than you.

Chaplains are full-time public safety professionals. However it should be noted that sacred writings and a spiritual motivation reside at the very heart of all chaplaincy. The reason we choose to minister to the incarcerated is *because of* our deeply-felt religious beliefs.

Prison chaplaincy is a sacred, spiritual ministry. Though the approach of this booklet is practical, it must be plainly stated that facility chaplaincy is never to be entered into as "a job." Chaplaincy is a service that carries sacred trusts and practices that are best reflected upon and revisited continually.

In fact, the safest and best thing for you will be to earn a reputation for having strong religious convictions, and standards, and beliefs. Staff and inmates will be looking to see if you are credible; and knowledgeable about your religion, and about theirs. They will watch to learn if you are consistent, and if your faith in what you believe is real and sincere.

Inside the prisons you will be earning whatever reputation, or prison "jacket," that you live out on a daily basis. If you live out your faith well, and especially if you take time to gain a strong skill in religious literacy of the other faiths, and live out your faith with honest conviction, you will become a skilled prison chaplain.

At the same time, prison administration may or may not be supportive of clergy or spiritually-driven persons being on staff inside a prison. Tensions may exist if management is especially non-religious, or biased. Don't clash with them, but use this as a time to investigate your own religious beliefs and sacred writings.

Conversely, support for what you do may increase among staff members who support you in your spirituality or spiritual work, especially as you earn staff's trust through your reliability and your consistency and your communications.

At the same time, some staff members who have strong religious affiliations may question why you spend so much time with inmates instead of staff.

Other staff might ask how you can live with yourself or sleep at night when you allow or protect the presence and practice of other religions. How will you answer?

In light of today's multi-faith society, your commitment to the duty to serve inside today's multi-faith prisons needs to be felt spiritually and deeply in order to stay the course.

Both staff members and inmates may come privately to a chaplain asking spiritual questions. One of the greatest heartaches you might face may be that, unlike other types of chaplaincies, you may be granted little time to interact with the spiritual needs of prison staff. Your assigned position may be designated for inmates. How will you respond?

Consider yourself blessed and fortunate if you are granted the privilege of taking part in emergency support teams for staff, for tending to hospitalized staff, or responding to employee family crises or death. These times will be rich.

In the correctional culture chaplains and religious program coordinators may be increasingly more likely to be hired to tend to inmates rather than to staff.

Your heart may ache as staff needs might increasingly go unmet. A sad reality might be that one day you might not be allowed enough time in the day to spend with staff—not on the clock, anyway. What will you do?

Regardless of the ever-changing multi-faith organizational world, a chaplain must never lose sight of why they believe what they believe. In the face of diverse religions, the facility chaplain holds a duty to operate in a manner that is well-informed in their own faith, and continually introspective of their own religious convictions.

Yet you can never push your faith on others in the multi-faith prison. To serve as chaplain you must make a commitment to provide spiritual care such as grief counseling to inmates from every faith group equally, regardless of their professed faith or yours.

Perhaps you will be blessed to be able to preach, and lead worship, and teach, depending upon the particular setting that you join. Some prisons may have religious volunteers do all these clergy ritual tasks.

Still, the more strongly you hold to your faith, the better spiritual care provider you will be towards everyone. This commitment to compassionate care really can't be understood until you start to actually live it out inside today's multi-faith prison culture.

At the same time, always keep in mind that in the multi-faith prison culture you can never put down or ridicule other religions in your interactions. If you are fortunate enough to officiate as clergy during religious rituals and services in today's correctional setting, you can never ridicule other faiths in your teaching.

No matter what faith tradition you profess, ridicule is prohibited by policy in the multi-faith prison setting. You will do well to respect this reality if you plan to remain a prison chaplain.

But it is time to shift gears a bit. Like every day within the duties of prison work, we must always tend to the practical things.

For that reason, this pocket contains more than our thoughts and feelings and spiritual backgrounds. Like everything in the prisons, this pocket also has a very practical daily use. Reaching deeper into this jacket pocket, the hand comes across…polarized sunglasses. What is the need for those in a prison?

Again, polarized sunglasses or "clip-ons" are purely an option to you as a worker, even if in your prison facility sunglasses are allowed at all. If you can use sunglasses in your prison, they may hold benefit to the facility chaplain who treks regularly between buildings.

Here sunglasses or clip-on sunglasses are one option for safely optimizing the sudden transition in lighting from very bright spaces to darker spaces, and vice versa.

Why is this practical? You may need to be able to very quickly transition in visibility when moving from a bright outdoors religious ceremony into the chapel or a living unit.

How do sunglasses matter? Again, can you safely afford to be blinded, either by sudden light, or by sudden darkness?

Clip-on sunglasses go on or come off at the precise moment you transition from light to dark, or from inside a building to outside in the bright sun. Again, check your local facility rules.

Does this reference to lightness and darkness have a religious connotation or a spiritual undertone? No, not religious, just the potential for a practical discussion about personal safety inside the prisons.

A great prayer for a prison chaplain is to have "a sharp eye, a thick skin, and a soft heart." The ability to transition safety and quickly from outdoors to indoors by changing out sunglasses or clip-ons is just one practical idea to help you potentially keep "a sharp eye."

Remember, in the correctional culture, safety and security always comes first. Safety and security is the first and foremost mindset of all prisons workers, including chaplains and religious program administrative assistants:

> Chaplains…must use spiritual discernment to balance religious needs and security. Truly, with prison staff, everyone is security…no matter what the job title. Security is the bottom line in every activity or program, even religious services. Every competent chaplain understands that without safety, programs cannot exist.[3]

That prayer was for "a sharp eye, a thick skin, and a soft heart." A prison chaplain who prays for "a sharp eye" finds value in the ability to quickly make the transition between outside and in. The quick transition from light to dark may help avoid a dangerous blind spot.

---

[3] Judith Coleman, "Chaplains: God's Partners In Prison" *Corrections Today 65,* no. 7 (December 2003), 122.

Working inside prisons likely involves potential dangers, and you will never be without personal risk in corrections culture. Don't underestimate the benefit of simple precautions.

Are sunglasses required? Of course not, just like the metaphor of a jacket is not required; but are sunglasses a good idea? Remember, you may want sunglasses to provide coverage for religious services held outside. Sunglasses are practical when you stand outside for long periods of time monitoring outdoor rituals for Native American religions, or any of a number of different Pagan religions who require seasonal outdoor services, such as Wicca, Druid, and Asatru.

This brings up an important point about providing religious services for religions with small numbers of participants.

Volunteers from the community help by supervising such specialized services, especially those outside the faith tradition of the chaplain. But what about when there are no volunteers available for that religion?

Some prisons have policies that prohibit inmates from gathering for religious rituals unless an appropriate volunteer from that religion is present. In these jurisdictions, those inmates may never get services or activities.

When volunteer sponsorship is not available from the outside community, you should think about monitoring these rituals yourself, so that the inmates can gather to practice their religion.

Prison legal and grievance departments are grateful for prison workers who consistently demonstrate competency in coordinating and scheduling religious events and services. This becomes increasingly important as inmate religious complaints gain ground under federal legislation such as RLUIPA.

If you choose to supervise religions in which you are not knowledgeable, you first need to learn the basics about those religions. Why is this? Imagine being surrounded by skilled manipulators, which in most prison settings happens continually.

Next, imagine them asking you to allow them to practice a religion which has rituals and customs that may sound odd or suspicious to you, from the perspective of facility safety and security.

How can you determine if their requested rituals are legitimate if you do not understand their terminology and their religion to some level?

You do not have to change your religion, or violate your personal spirituality. You do not have to practice another religion, but you will have to gain religious literacy and skill in understanding what is actually needed for numerous other religious rituals and practices.

It will be needed to carefully think through the basic ritual and literature needs of each religion, and do some research on the validity of requests for religious expression.

Develop a fair and consistent method for scheduling and announcing religious services, and for tracking attendance. The time you spend serving these needs will be time well spent, as these needs not only benefit the incarcerated by protect the institution as well.

Tracking complex religious schedules will take time. If you have a good administrative assistant, as I have been blessed to have over the years, you will operate at a tremendous advantage. At the same time the chaplain, and every prison religious program worker, is encouraged to become some of the most computer-competent persons on the prison staff.

And again that prayer: ask for "a sharp eye, a thick skin, and a soft heart."

Discussion Segment Two Questions

1. Think of the different people you have known in your circle of friends, or at work, in your neighborhood, at school, or in other social settings. What role does spirituality or religion play in their lives, especially when crisis or difficulty comes? How might religious expression or spiritual activities and rituals potentially help the incarcerated to cope?
2. Your duty for public safety is in balance with your own safety, as well as staff safety. How would you provide for diverse religious freedom if you encounter a situation where the religious ceremonies or beliefs compete or clash, and the inmates are angry with you or with other inmates?
3. Imagine yourself as the mediator in the above scene; if you have enough time and staff, have each group act out a role-play to such a situation.

4. How can you learn about potential safety and security risks that may be associated with diverse religious groups that may seek to operate within your facility?[4]

---

[4] Retired prison chaplain Peter Grant supplies details on STGs, saying that he himself has been threatened, Grant, *Walls, Wire, Bars and Souls*, 86-103. It may be helpful to familiarize yourself with publications such as Timothy G. Baysinger, "Right-wing Group Characteristics and Ideology," July 2006, https://www.hsaj.org/articles/166, or Mark S. Hamm, "Prisoner Radicalization: Assessing the Threat in U. S. Correctional Facilities," October 27, 2008, NIJ Journal No. 261, http://www.nij.gov/journals/261/pages/prisoner-radicalization.aspx.

DISCUSSION SEGMENT THREE

A Heart For Service

Your heart should care deeply about the correctional facility's needs, ranging from safety to security to smooth and orderly operations.

The duty for religious provision leads to this next pocket continuously throughout the day and throughout the week. This pocket is perhaps the most important and the most frequently-accessed pocket of all from a facility operations perspective.

This pocket bulges with important paperwork. The contents of this pocket help keep your prison safe from unrest caused by a potential lack of religious freedom. In this pocket are religious service and event planning calendars, callout schedules, radio call signs and phone numbers, and serious illness reports.

Serious illness reports track those inmates whose deaths are expected within a relatively short period of time due to irreversible illness. The chaplain must remain in relationship with these individuals, tending to their spiritual needs.

The chaplain must stay in communication with inmates' family members as death approaches, even if the call comes to you in the middle of the night. These are times when clergy really help provide compassionate care.

As spiritual care provider to the prisoners, the chaplain may hold the memorial service for inmates, as their spiritual caregiver. Again, do not force your religious views into this service, rather consider honoring the dead civilly and respectfully through a religious ritual that will help make meaning and bring healing.

Likewise, think ahead of time how you might inform an inmate sensitively when their loved ones call with news of a hospitalization or death of a family member. This is often a heartbreaking matter for an incarcerated parent of a child who dies. At these times all your best counseling and compassionate care skills will be put to use in a meaningful and supportive, caring, personalized way. This will mean a lot to the incarcerated, and to the prison staff who watch over them.

Many such calls come unexpected, but for the most part your counseling schedule may be pre-arranged through the callout schedule. The callout schedule can work in some ways like a clergy or counselor or minister's appointment log. Callouts may include requests for help with family needs, pastoral counseling, theological inquiries, preparation for baptism or marriage, or resolving religious disputes at the lowest level possible.

Like your compassionate care of those who experience massive disruptions to their lives through family losses, your willingness to reflectively hear and credibly resolve religious disputes with fairness and equity will help and benefit both the incarcerated individual and the orderly operations of the facility and the agency.

Inmates also ask to be called out to discuss and request new religious activities, or add new types of religious rituals or services. Here religious literacy is a priceless tool. And, the chaplain benefits if their facility chain of command provides standardized written policy and a process for consistent, fair, just evaluation of requests for new religious services.

Inmates increasingly request appointments to request religious property. It is helpful to remember that from the point of view of the incarcerated, property of any kind is rare and treasured during their time in prison, where all personal belongings are sparse and far between. Your time may increasingly be spent responding to requests for religious artifacts, spiritual talismans, and deity images or sacred icons from diverse religious perspectives. Incarcerated individuals may feel very strongly and may need attentive clergy involvement.

An important word here is fitting about counseling the incarcerated. By now you have heard that inmates may still have "rough edges." They may at times follow past life-patterns of manipulating and such. In due time, this will be no surprise to you—just a part of prison work.

However, none of these "rough edges" matter when an incarcerated person needs your sacred spiritual help as a chaplain. Here you must have the pre-disposed heart and mindset to instantly "forget the past" and be a fully-engaged, fully-involved, fully-caring active empathetic listener.

Even if an incarcerated had recently threatened you and you had him or her locked up for it; if he or she calls for a chaplain to help them, even in a segregation or maximum-security cell, go to their window and interact with compassion and active listening.

At that moment their needs are indescribably vital to them, and so are you as their chaplain. Compassionate care is crucial.

When inmates know you will drop everything and care compassionately for them in their crisis situation, then your "jacket" or reputation as a chaplain will truly be well-lived out.

Make the arrangements with staff to get to these counseling interventions as soon as you can. Staff will be extremely grateful to have a chaplain who actively cares about the inmates' spiritual and emotional needs, and a chaplain who can be relied on to help staff respond to the emotionally-distraught incarcerated individuals.

Custody staff whose posts interact with the incarcerated each of the twenty-four hours of the day in the living units will be especially grateful for help you can give to counsel the incarcerated, as will be their sergeants, as well as their shift commanders who may at times be the ones who first receive the calls from inmates' family members in times of deaths in the family or other crises.

To make these types of connections with staff, and for countless other reasons related to facility operations and facility safety and security, radio call signs and phone numbers are essential and necessary for operating inside a prison. Memorize important phone numbers and radio call signs. If you carry them in your pocket, be careful not to let phone lists get into an inmate's hands.

Doors will need to open as a prison religious employee travels widely throughout the facility, such as when counseling or responding to religious disputes or investigating inmate complaints.

Providing death notifications and responding to staff requests to help an inmate— in all these types of prison clergy situations and more, staff radios and the worksite phones are needed to open the doors to inmate living units; and religious clergy might be asked to visit inmates who work any of numerous job locations within some types of prison operations.

Radios also help prison religious program staff – whether chaplains or administrative assistants or religious program coordinators or by any title– become aware of emergencies that may delay or prevent access to areas of the facility. Specialized training in handling emergencies will be provided to you, and must be carefully followed and obeyed.

Communication is the life's blood of the prison, and a chaplain must develop and maintain a diverse communication network with staff in every area in order to be effective. And while inside the prison, remember that all prison workers are responsible for each others' safety.

Discussion Segment Three Questions

1. How important is careful appointment scheduling in your prior school, work or civic commitments? What makes scheduling easier? What makes it difficult?
2. Think of a time when you lost a loved one. Now imagine not being able to respond when to a family crisis. How would this feel? How would you react?
3. Have you ever utilized the services of a counselor, minister, or spiritual advisor? How might interventions help "keep the peace" in a prison?

DISCUSSION SEGMENT FOUR
The Religious Calendar

Good teamwork and communications are the life's blood of a prison facility. But for the prison religious program, its flesh and bone so to speak are its religious services, religious events, sacred rituals, and special spiritual activities.

The chaplain, in caring for persons of a wide divergence of religious beliefs and practices, needs to understand and care for the persons in each of those religions, even if not fully understanding the deeper doctrines of those religions.

For this reason, the religious calendar tucked away for easy access in the jacket pocket deserves a close look, and certainly deserves a Discussion Segment of its own.

Looking out for others means looking ahead. For a prison religious program worker, looking ahead means having insight into the physical celestial realities of the sun and moon.

One could say that all religions—not just Pagan or Native American—look to nature in one way or another.[5] An experienced chaplain recognizes that a great many religious observances center upon celestial realities, especially around the annual cycle of the sun and the lunar cycle of the moon.

Solar and lunar cycles make the job of planning and coordinating your facility religious program calendar straightforward, somewhat predictable, and very achievable. You will be successful if you begin by drafting your religious calendar based on recognizing the pattern of equinoxes and solstices, especially the Spring equinox.

The Spring equinox brings into view a chaplain's challenge to prioritize and balance the needs of Native American ways, and all the Christian faiths, as well as Judaism, Islam, Paganism, and other beliefs.

---

[5] According to field observations among prison religious by the author, aboriginal religions with roots on different continents, such as Native American relative to North America, Druid for central Europe, and Asatru for Norse or Teutonic regions, tend to personify and venerate seasons of the year. Worship may be based on agrarian cycles and seasonal activities necessary for survival. In this way the religious calendar of some religions is based on deep-seated and passionately-held values which seek protection from the elements, and provision of sustenance for tribes and races.

To gain insight into many of the world's religions, start by listening to the thoughts of your inmate planning teams related to their rituals based around the Spring full moon. The Spring full moon is a great place to dive into religious literacy.

Ask your religious volunteers—or if you are certain you can knowledgeably and safely manage them, inmate planning teams—what the equinoxes and solstices mean to their faith, and be wise enough to listen as you plan your events and activities.

If you do not have the appropriate religious volunteers to advise you on their specific faith group needs, consider screening and selecting a separate inmate planning team for each particular faith group. Beware that if inmates with mixed motives gain inroads, such a planning team may at times have a potential to seek to mislead you for their own purposes. If you choose to use inmate planning teams, you can check to verify their claims with outside authorities for that religion.

You may find that Spring brings hope of new life or of sustained life to the majority of the world's religions. To build the calendar for a prison religious program, it is valuable to let the Spring equinox be the starting point.[6]

We think of our year as Spring, Summer, Autumn, and Winter. Of these, almost every religion in the prisons will require some sort of a Spring full-moon related event, so it is good to start with the most difficult time of year first, then sort out the rest of the religious calendar year.

Let me say that again: almost every religion in your prison will require some sort of a Spring full-moon timing-related ritual. How is that possible? Is this true?

Yes, almost every religion in your prison will require some sort of a Spring full-moon timing-related ritual. Some of the more widely known are Easter, Passover, the Native American Change of Seasons. Others include Wicca, Druid, Asatru. Within Christianity, specific groups have their own necessary dates.

---

[6] Regarding the connotation, "Spring," NASA describes a year on earth as being divided into four quarters, or seasons – spring, summer, autumn (fall), and winter, see Sandra May, "Season," July 22, 2015, http://www.nasa.gov/audience/forstudents/k-4/dictionary/Season.html. Of course the meteorological or weather patterns differs between northern and southern hemisphere. This book utilizes northern hemisphere terminology, specifically that of the west.

To practice seeing how this religious calendar works, start by using a neutral and very reliable source to verify the Spring equinox date that will come during March of next year.[7] Type this date into a computer table or spreadsheet.

While you are at it, type in also the dates of the autumnal equinox that occurs in September, and the dates of the two solstices: June and December. Accurate, reliable specific dates are needed as your religious program calendar builds. These will impact every religion.

To help keep these clear in your mind, perhaps think of the word "equinox" as "equal." At the "equinox" most areas of the earthly globe have "equal" lengths of light and dark hours.

Spring and autumn days have nearly "equal" hours of daylight and night on the "equinox."

Many religions will need to share these days for religious rituals and gatherings. They "compete" so to speak, for the same days.

But different religions celebrate these Change of Seasons differently. They also

---

[7]http://aa. usno. navy. mil/data/docs/EarthSeasons. php.

compete, one might say, for space and time at the Spring equinox. Again, these include Native American as well as Pagan Wicca, Druid, and Asatru.

In light of the American Indian Religious Freedom Act (AIRFA) and Religious Land Use and Institutionalized Persons Act (RLUIPA),[8] it is wise to grant priority to the Native American Change of Seasons ceremony for every equinox and every solstice, if a facility has a Native American population.

In the Spring, it is wise to allow the Native American population to celebrate in the day or days immediately before the Spring equinox, as opposed to after. You can work with your Native American planning team inmates members to ascertain what is necessary.

Next, choose and type in Spring equinox ceremony dates and times for Pagan Asatru, Wicca, and Druid.

---

[8] The Religious Land Use and Institutionalized Persons Act (RLUIPA), passed in 2000, gave teeth to the American Indian Religious Freedom Act (AIRFA) of 1978, and expanded religious freedom for all faith groups. This legislation opens doors for religious expression in the prisons. In a nutshell, RLUIPA requires the prison facility to consider every request for religious expression.

Your Wicca planning teams may describe this festival to You as Ostara. They have a more clear understanding than you as to how Ostara culturally and historically became "Easter" for much of society.

These Ostara ceremonies should occur within the seven days prior to the Spring—sometimes also thought of as vernal—equinox, or on the day of the equinox.

Asatru and some forms of Druidry will also have their own specialized names for their own religious rituals for the change of seasons times of solstices and equinoxes. Here your inmate planning teams will be of tremendous help in scheduling.

Again, you do not have to believe what others believe, but you must provide fairly and justly for their freedom of religious expression. Take time for religious literacy and you will become a skilled chaplain or religious program coordinator or administrative assistant.

Inquire and learn whether agency policy or facility operating rules limits these activities, for instance if they can take place with suitable pre-approved volunteers.

Let's get back to our making our religious calendar. As a general rule, Easter Sunday in Western culture falls on the first Sunday after the first full moon of after the Paschal Equinox. Usually, but not always, this is the first Sunday after the Spring equinox. Again, verify your dates with an original, reliable source, being cautious to not use un-verified web sources.

It is traditionally preferable to place any requested special Easter gatherings or Paschal observances just before this date. Remember that Western and Eastern religious Easter dates may be up to a month apart.

Next, schedule and type in ritual gatherings for Jewish inmates for Passover, in case you have or might receive Jewish inmates. Passover Seder observances for the Jews will be in the evenings of the first two nights of Passover. Again, these dates will change every year, so a reliable source is vital.

It may feel odd to think that Passover, which Biblically leads into Easter, might fall after Easter Sunday because the lunar Jewish calendar typically varies from the solar calendar that sets the date for Easter. Again, be careful to use only reliable sources.

As you type in your ritual dates for Passover, use this as an opportunity to grow in religious literacy. It is vitally important to learn and to understand and to remember that Jewish holidays and rituals – like Muslim holidays and rituals – begin at sundown the night before. This skill in religious literacy will prevent lawsuits and will greatly help you to "shop ahead" for the ritual foods and items necessary for good Passover Seder celebrations.

It may be helpful to keep in mind that Jewish prison populations may be small in size but big in legal clout. This can be true of other religious groups as well. The chaplain can help protect the legal resources of the correctional facility by providing all inmates freedom of religious expression.

Here your devotion to gaining religious literacy will make you an effective, trustworthy chaplain, as the Jewish calendar date of 14 Nisan signals the start of Passover, and also signals a Christian event. Many may not know that the Spring equinox has the one time of year that the Jehovah's Witness religion and its Watchtower celebrants have a mandatory ritual event. The WatchTower participants will not practice Easter, and will not practice Christmas, but they must practice gathering for religious ritual for "The Lord's Evening Meal," or communion, at the precise time of the Spring equinox.

Again, to practice accuracy in your religious literacy you must use accurate dates for your timing and your planning. Use your Jehovah's Witness inmate planning team, and you will gain their respect and avoid lawsuits at the same time. A skilled chaplain will speak with local Watchtower representatives to be sure of the exact date for the Lords' Evening Memorial. Coordinate the date carefully with the Jehovah's Witness inmate planning team.

Here your commit to grow in religious literacy will be vital to success, as the time of day for the Watchtower Society's ritual is vastly different from the timing for Muslim or Jewish rituals. You will learn from your local Watchtower that this Jehovah's Witness ceremony **cannot begin until after dark**.

Perhaps you can see why the Spring equinox is a great launching point for your religious calendar. Blessedly, the rest of the calendar is simple by comparison!

Now is an excellent time to type in each of the change of season dates for Native American and Pagan practitioners, again on or just before each solstice and equinox: Spring, summer, autumn (fall), and winter.

Type each of these into your computer table or spreadsheet, along with the mid-quarter observance dates for the Pagan Wicca, Druid, and Asatru religious ritual calendars. Every year these Pagan midpoint ritual dates arrive on roughly February 02, May 01, August 01, and October 31.

Your inmate planning teams and practitioners will respect you if you speak with them, and try to schedule ceremonies on or in the few days just before these dates whenever possible, in contrast to after.[9]

Work closely with your inmate planning teams for each faith group. They will be glad to provide you with the details and the evidence related to the validity of these dates and observances.

As you grow in these skills, your reputation, your prison "jacket," will become that of someone who cares for the sacred and spiritual

---

[9] According to field observations of the author, Asatruar may ask to celebrate Frefaxi around August 27 or 28, instead of August 01; and Asatru Winter Nights around October 17, instead of October 31.

religious and ritual needs of others who believe vastly different from yourself. Your dedication to growing in your religious literacy will contribute to the orderly operations of the facility, and will help keep you safe.

Inmates of every faith group will see what is happening, that they are being cared for by their chaplain. They will respect you, and they will respect and honor your own personally-held religious beliefs and convictions.

Congratulations, your facility's religious calendar is almost done.

Write in Christmas for the various Christians, and perhaps write in a Spring date such as Buddha's Birthday for a Buddhist celebration. Add the nineteen day Bahai "The Fast" that occurs immediately before the Spring equinox, and the end is almost there.

You've done a great job in growing in religious literacy, even in this short time! Please believe me when I say you will make a big difference in managing the religious program of your prison. You will see.

Now, it is time for one last "growth spurt" in your advances in multi-faith religious literacy.

Now it's time to pre-plan and schedule the religious fasting dates and special religious meal dates for the diverse religious groups under your care.

Within Islam specifically, it's time to schedule Ramadan. Again, the required Ramadan ritual days are forecast and easily accessible from Muslim authorities and sources. Again, work with your Muslim inmate planning team to ensure you and they are anticipating the same time frames for each particular religious year's observances. The more diligent you are as facility chaplain or religious program coordinator or administrative assistant, the fewer tensions you will have when your facility's group of religiously passionate Muslim inmates goes for one month not eating any food during the daylight hours. Welcome to Ramadan—you can do it!

Here religious literacy means knowing that the Muslim Ramadan fasting dates change every year. The Islamic ritual fasting reflects the 10-11 days that the Islamic calendar moves forward every year relative to the solar calendar.

Plan the Ramadan fast well in advance, so that your facility can arrange for the specialized religious foods necessary.

Even "knowing" the approximate dates is not enough, with Ramadan, as the actual starting dates is widely in dispute within the Muslim communities themselves, as are the "methods for sighting the moon." Your best bet is to check with authoritative Islamic websites, and listen to your planning team to learn the importance of local sightings of the moon by Islamic officials.

As you begin to wrap up your religious calendar, be careful to pre-plan and to type in the dates for the Muslim ritual gathering services and events for Eid al Fitr and Eid al Adha. Your planning team will teach you what these are, though you will need to verify the extent of the rituals. In a nutshell, these are ritual group prayer dates, which require early-morning prayer gatherings on specific, non-interchangeable dates.

Religious literacy about Judaism, and providing for religious fasting for Jewish observances can become a bit more varied than perhaps any other religion. Judaism, along with the Messianic Judaism that observes Jewish time frames, celebrates seven key fasts during the year, along with certain specifically-timed holiday observances.

Remember that these dates change every year. As with all your religious calendar needs, find a reliable Jewish source, such as Aleph Institute, and type in these important dates, remembering that in Judaism a day begins at sundown the evening before.

The facility's religious calendar is nearly complete. If the institution holds a Hispanic Catholic population, a priest is needed to provide an "Our Lady of Guadalupe" Spanish-speaking Mass on or just before December 12 each year.

What if these observances conflict with a state or federal holiday? It is likely the facility chaplain must adjust their own personal life and schedule to meet the needs of those they serve.

When the start or end to Ramadan falls on a federal holiday or on your weekend, be sure to be onsite so as to help the facility meet this need. It may help to think of this as being somewhat like an overseas mission, where the missionary cannot be home for the holidays.

If the facility supports an annual religious event calendar, perhaps where family members can attend a religious event and share a meal, type in seasonal dates that honor the group's religious calendars.

For example, a Christian family dinner event might be ideal just before Easter, while a Pagan feast event may fall near Samhain, or what you might know as Halloween.

A Muslim feast event may be best near the time of the Hajj, which again moves forward 10-11 days every solar year.

Again, provide for religious needs without showing favoritism either towards or against any religious faith. It is not your place to either favor or to ridicule a religion.

Congratulations! You have now built a viable religious calendar by which to manage your facility's religious program activities, including the needs of your minority religions.

Well done! As you show this commitment year after year, your reputation and your prison "jacket" will become that of someone who is competent, reliable, caring, involved; a good listener, open to others' feelings and beliefs; devoted, empathetic, and engaged. Your religious calendar might just surprise you as your most practical way of living out the very values that you studied in order to become a chaplain. You may be actively living out the things you value the most. And in committing to do this well, you will certainly gain the respect of prison administration, custody staff, and the incarcerated and their families.

Like most of prison work, the religious calendar is not easy. Even more, your number of activities must be multiplied by two if you are the chaplain for two perimeters,[10] and by three if three perimeters, and so on. It is not unheard of to coordinate schedules for up to six or seven prison populations, all competing for the chaplain's time and for specific, necessary dates for their religious observances.

Still, with a commitment to growing in religious literacy, and a little practice, you will have this down to a science in no time.

As you work hard on this religious calendar, please know: it cannot be overstated that your commitment to care for the inmates of every faith group and to provide well for them goes a long way to keeping the peace and security at your prison.

---

[10] Think of a "perimeter" as the fence around a portion of the prison. Different custody levels are commonly situated adjacent to one another within separately fenced perimeters of a single prison facility.

Of course the communication skill sets are vital for managing a prison religious program. A part of your commitment includes creating and posting flyers about these sacred ritual and religious fast dates, times, and spiritual observances. These are posted for inmate viewing in the chapel or religious activities centers, and in each inmate living unit.

Here your computer and communication skills are valuable. You may want to include instructions to inmates as to how to sign up to attend these special services and seasonal activities. Deadline dates for sign-up are essential for ordering ritual supplies and specialized sacred religious food items.

From this calendar of annual events and major seasonal festivals, you are now able to insert time frames for the weekly religious services that you officiate or monitor, including monitoring religious gatherings for minority religions for which no volunteer or sponsor can be found from the community.

You do not need to teach these other religious tenets, but you need to get them a room and the supplies and literature they need.

You may find yourself being responsible for coordinating rooms and materials for as many as a hundred religious services or gatherings per week. For this task you certainly need religious volunteers from the community.

Time spent recruiting and meeting with faith-based community organization representatives, whether clergy or lay, as well as ministry and spiritual care volunteers, will help tremendously.

You might supervise hundreds of religious volunteers from the outside spiritual communities. These take turns monitoring or conducting the vast majority of weekly religious activities. The value of these volunteers is impossible to overstate. The health of your religious program depends upon the diversity and commitment level of your religious volunteers.

Another word is appropriate at this point regarding what have been called "visiting ministers" of one type or another.

Tensions and resentments against you as facility chaplain will sometimes surface in the hearts and minds of religious volunteers or paid part-time visiting ministers. You may be thought of as favoring one group and restricting another.

One researcher described the feelings and perceptions of visiting ministers in this way:

> [Visiting ministers] must rely on full-time Christian chaplains to facilitate their access to prisoners, meeting rooms, and religious artifacts. This dependency gives rise to feelings of resentment, unjust discrimination, and marginalization among members of minority faith communities...in some cases the Visiting Ministers are only admitted to prisons if a Christian chaplain is present to vouch for them... [and] to negotiate with prison authorities for the use of meeting rooms, religious artefacts (sic), notice boards, as well as for the provision of special diets and religious holidays for minority faith prisoners. Not surprisingly, many Visiting Ministers reported that the opportunities available to them varied widely with the willingness of the local...chaplains to facilitate things for them and to act as "brokers" with prison managers. Some also objected to being made dependent on Christian chaplains by other prison staff...." Governors usually do not return my calls and always refer me to the chaplain—which I resent."[11]

That same research shows that most visiting ministers express satisfaction outwardly

---

[11] James A. Beckford, "Social Justice and Religion in Prison: The Case of England and Wales," Social Justice Research, 1999, Vol.12 (4), 318.

with the arrangements provided for their faith group, but inwardly often wish to gain more autonomy and access to the prison.[12]

An effective prison chaplain will try to do everything reasonable to gain the support and help of these visiting ministers, volunteers, and paid part-time religious service providers.

They cannot be expected to understand the complexities of your job as a staff member. As volunteers, or part-time contractors, they are likely to hold inaccurate perceptions about your own access to areas of the facility. Do not hold any of these perceptions against them, rather forgive.

Be grateful for their help, and always remember that religious volunteers and visiting ministers are one of the most crucial ingredients to a healthy religious program in today's correctional setting.

Do everything you can to provide fairly and justly for minority religions and diverse denominations. Still, do not be taken aback by expressions of "resentment and feelings of

---

[12] Beckford, "Social Justice," 318.

injustice."[13] You will never be unable to avoid all complaints or allegations, no matter how fair and just you are. Only do not let the charges be true.

Remember that your sacred spiritual duty as a clergy or religious worker is a high calling. Do the best you can, and when resentments come against you—and they will—forgive quickly; and continue to provide for people fairly, justly, and consistently.

Discussion Segment Four Questions

1. Discuss four things about Spring equinox.
2. What questions has this new information raised in your mind about the different world religions?
3. Should every request for religious expression be granted? Why or why not? What might be some implications for facility scheduling and planning?
4. List three things you learned about Judaism and/or Islam from this Segment.
5. Why might it be important to provide for these religions in the prisons?

---

[13] Beckford, "Social Justice," 319.

6. What percentage of today's world globally do you think currently observes Islam or Judaism?

DISCUSSION SEGMENT FIVE
Simple Respect: Part One

The next pocket of the metaphor of "A Chaplain's Prison Jacket" is the left side pocket. What are the contents of this pocket? In this pocket is handful of clean non-latex non-hypoallergenic work gloves. What are the gloves for, with a sacred or spiritual religious program?

Every prison worker stands ready to respond to inmate illnesses and injuries, where blood or bodily fluids are bound to be encountered eventually – especially when dealing with potentially violent inmates. But fights are ideally not the norm in prison, so why would a religious program specialist carry plastic gloves?

First, gloves are mandatory in the sense of Universal Precautions. Though this is a medical term, the chaplain or religious program coordinator or administrative assistant is a prison worker with a general duty and responsibility to be aware of infectious disease control guidelines, and to be mindful to prevent spread.

Another religious literacy skill set that cannot be encouraged enough is the skill of handling inmates' religious artifacts and sacred ritual articles with special respect.

Do not be surprised when an inmate feels aghast or degraded whenever items the inmate thinks of as deeply sacred are touched or handled by someone of another faith.

Pagan religious practitioners may feel strongly that your spiritual "energy" may taint their sacred item. Likewise, Native Americans consider eagle feathers as deeply sacred and deeply spiritual. A habit of "gloving up" prior to handling such items shows respect for the inmate's beliefs, and helps protect the facility from unnecessary complaints and grievances.

You may want to ask the inmate to show you the item, or request permission from the inmate to move or handle their sacred artifacts. Gloves protect both the worker and the facility while also showing respect for religious and sacred items that inmates may deem require special handling.

It is wise for the chaplain to keep in mind that religion inside the prisons is a potentially contentious issue, as inmates may become quite agitated if their sense of religious allegiance and sacred or spiritual expression feel offended.

Something as simple and practical as using clean gloves can take you farther than you realize, whether in keeping the gloves "spiritually clean" and uncontaminated out of religious respect for handling sacred items, or in responding to Infectious Disease Control situations. And in the very practical sense, gloves are a respectful precaution to consider when preparing the juice and crackers for the sacred ritual of communion.

Fresh gloves especially come out when food handling safety is in view. Examples are the serving of food at religious special events, and the preparation of sacred ceremonial elements such as Buddhist TSOG elements.

Gloves also serve as personal protective equipment for a religious program worker. Gloves can be a PPE precaution when cleaning everything from the sweat lodge to the baptistery.

If you've never worked in a prison before, you will be astounded when you see the number of boxes of gloves used by prison staff in a typical week.

Discussion Segment Five Questions

1. Describe a time when you were potentially exposed to infectious disease on the job—had you already received prior training in Infectious Disease Control, and if so, how did your training inform or alter your response?
2. How might a chaplain help restore the facility after a prison fight or riot?
3. Regarding the idea of showing respect for handling sacred items, why might an inmate become agitated if they feel their sacred items are mishandled? What might they do?
4. Imagine you are interacting with an inmate who has a history of violent behavior, how might they respond to a sense of their religious rights being violated?

DISCUSSION SEGMENT SIX
Simple Respect: Part Two

Perhaps the question lingers as to whether or not to wear an actual jacket, and if one is worn, what would it look like. After all, some might look upon a person in a jacket as being an uptight or stuffy person. Again the "jacket" is just a metaphor for your outward reputation of consistency, professionalism, reliability, including a clear commitment to the sacred nature of the religious program.

Continuing on with the "jacket" metaphor, let's continue to explore the practical aspects of serving as a prison religious worker. Practicality always has its benefits. Reaching over to another jacket pocket leads to items that serve a combination of needs—both practical and revered.

Two plastic bags are there. The first bag is immensely practical. This bag holds some adhesive bandage strips. Nicks and cuts can happen anywhere in the chaplain's life, from causes ranging from paper cuts, to scrapes from handling tools and materials, to the unexpected. As a chaplain you won't always be around a first aid kit, and it's handy to have a few band-aids.

Given the tendency of prisons to run high rates of infectious disease, quick first aid is practical and necessary. A good general rule is that any broken skin a prison worker has should remain covered while inside the prison.

If the skin was broken offsite from non-work activities such as hobbies or sports, the little baggie of small adhesive bandages still comes in handy to quickly change a loose or wet band-aid.

The second baggie in this right side pocket is religious in nature. It contains a book of matches. A chaplain may be the primary or only source for inmates to light their weekly religious ritual Sabbath and Catholic Mass candles. Pagan inmates need matches to light their sacred herbs and candles, and the outdoor ritual fires you scheduled in your religious calendar.

Continuing to grow in religious literacy, your Buddhist inmates need matches to light their sacred incense at the weekly rituals. Native Americans and Pagans alike must light their smudge shells and bowls. The prison chaplain does not have to agree with the religious significance of such spiritual rituals that others feel are sacred, but must provide dry, clean matches.

That is where the protective plastic baggie helps. A baggie holds matchbooks and at the same time provides protection from the weather, as these observances at times take the chaplain and the faith group outdoors to the "sacred grounds" where participants hold some of the rituals necessary to their faith.

Lighting of matches and candles for other faith groups is a good illustration of balancing the practical and the need for religious literacy in today's multi-faith prison culture. Despite the long hours utilizing computer skills and technology to develop your religious calendar, prison chaplaincy is not purely an indoor calling, and at times you will need to be outdoors.

Whether lighting a Sabbath "servant" candle or handing matches to a Druid or Wiccan inmate to light their fire or sacred incense, one rule is crucial in the multi-faith prison culture: just light it.

Do not favor one religion over another, and do not proselytize or ridicule. Never.

As part of the commitment to religious literacy, the chaplain learns how to become open to how to adequately serve inmates' needs, without judging their beliefs. Again, you do not need to believe what they believe, or support what they believe, but you will need to honor their right to believe and practice their faith.

A good rule here is to listen carefully to your inmate planning teams, and to check everything out through valid, reliable sources. And in order to be successful and effective as a prison chaplain you must "never neglect or bargain away a valid interest."

Keep in mind that diversity between religions need not foster outright debate. A chaplain should never be insensitive. Even unwittingly or unintentionally offending a religious belief may result in legal action.

Likewise it may help consider how an inmate who has serious mental illness might respond to ridicule or mocking, especially of a personally-vested area such as their religious beliefs.

Perhaps think through ahead of time how a person with a life sentence, or who feels they have "nothing to lose", may act out if they feel that one of his or her few freedoms in their life is being threatened, or ridiculed, or mocked.

Prison religious chaplaincy, done well, prevents trouble and helps provide for safety and security of the overall prison facility and the prison's workers and its incarcerated.

Discussion Segment Six Questions

1. Is lighting a sacred candle for someone of another religion the same as participating in that religious belief? Why or why not?
2. What are some ways to be professional towards other religious beliefs without compromising your own religious belief?
3. What could go wrong if prison religion is ridiculed or scorned, or not provided?

DISCUSSION SEGMENT SEVEN
Part of a Uniform?

This duty to protect safety and security within the prison raises the question "What type should the jacket be, if I am to wear an actual jacket?" Without entering too deeply into this potential debate, recognize that some clergy may tend toward a religious identifier such as a clerical collar or religious headgear. Others may avoid religious identifiers altogether, so as to not be stereotyped in some unintended way.

As with any and everything about prison life, you might ask yourself "What are the safety and security implications of my attire?"

For example, any prison worker who dresses in the same color or type of clothing as inmates creates unnecessary confusion and risk.

You may consider wearing clothing that is outwardly the same color as the custody staff uniform within your jurisdiction. For instance, if the officers in your prison all wear the color blue and all incarcerated inmates wear brown, you might choose to avoid brown. It may be a potential safety hazard to dress like inmates.

Regardless, a chaplain who outwardly looks and behaves consistently gains trust from prison custody staff. All custody staff tend to value consistency, and they value consistent behavior. Consistent attire may have the potential to help staff become familiar with who you are and how you think.

Either way, the "jacket" is not a fashion statement, it is purely practical. At the same time, it is good to be consistent and modest without being flashy or showy. This comes back to the idea of the reputation or *ethos* you will develop among coworkers and with inmates.

Again, in prison culture the term "jacket" brings to mind any of several diverse meanings. A jacket can be a "folder," a "past crime summary sheet," and most importantly a "reputation." Here the metaphor of a chaplain's prison jacket reaches a new depth of meaning because you are earning a reputation.

Prison workers are known to their peers by their actions, by their behavior, by their reputation, and even by their attire. The color of the jacket itself may speak volumes to staff and inmates about the perceived role, function, and attitude of the prison facility worker. For example, in emergency situations staff members need to be easily distinguishable from inmates.

The prison religious program worker who keeps this in mind, and who dresses professionally and consistently day in and day out, will find that their own movements in and through the prison compound will flow more smoothly, and as result will aid in the orderly operation of the facility they serve. Again, you do not need to wear a literal jacket. You do not need to be surrounded by literal pockets.

What about footwear? Footwear should be based on weather and on working conditions. For instance, when a chaplain is present during the mopping of linoleum floors in preparation for family religious services or food events, slippery floors require may slip-resistant soles.

Outdoor supervision of sacred religious gatherings during cold or rainy weather requires more substantial footwear. In many geographical regions, a thin jacket is not enough to protect and sustain the chaplain who travels among buildinʳ and monitors outdoor religious services. warmer garment is needed in many climates a weatherproof or water-repellent outer ʳ shell. A winter hat is crucial during parts of the year in the northern hemisphere.

Keep practicality in mind. Some days are cold enough to necessitate winter gloves. Zippered pockets keep these personal items from falling out around inmates, or from being pick-pocketed.

Again, does the color of clothing matter? Find out if your prison has guidelines for prohibited colors or styles of clothing and accessories. Remember that recognizable, consistent appearance can have its advantages. You cannot go wrong if you prioritize facility safety and security.

Think through each task in your role in the prisons, and find ways to provide "checks and balances" towards the safety of others. Develop a safety network, and talk continually with your coworkers. We are all in this correctional business together. Listen to the advice of other prison workers around you.

You do not need to buy clothing to succeed in your duties as a prison chaplain or chapel assistant or prison religious program worker. Remember, a "jacket" means more than a garment of clothing. The "jacket" is a metaphor for how you will become known and recognized within the prison setting.

Think through each aspect of why you do what you do. "A Chaplain's Prison Jacket" is a metaphor for your duty as you serve inside the prisons.

Discussion Segment Seven Questions

1. How important a factor is modesty in light of the potential for sexual attraction when working with sex offenders?
2. How will prison custody officers recognize who you are outwardly, so that they can have one less person to worry about as they carry out their duty for preserving public safety and for prison facility safety and security? Where will you adapt?
3. How will you become trustworthy and consistent in your interactions and dealings with prison line staff, custody officers and their sergeants, and with administration? What outward actions will shape your reputation?

4. You have heard it stated that attire is not the issue, but reputation and demeanor is. What about you? Will you commit to serve the spiritual needs of the prison culture well? Who will you choose to become as a public servant in today's multi-faith prison correctional culture?

DISCUSSION SEGMENT EIGHT

Pen and Paper

Though not part of the jacket itself, a shirt pocket is a great place to store a writing pen or two along with a notepad.

Why is a pen and a writing pad handy?

Many questions from staff come daily to a prison chaplain as he or she walks the facility. Writing down these questions and requests, along with a commitment to find out the answer, can go a long way towards keeping the peace. Prison staff is appreciative when a chaplain stops to write down a need, which later receives a follow-up conversation or email.

You might ask your facility staff if certain ink colors are prohibited for inmates. Perhaps you might not want to use inmate ink colors when signing forms or documents. And be sure to carefully track your own writing utensils. Imagine what something as simple as a staff member's writing pen can accomplish in the hands of a skilled forger.

Bear in mind, you will certainly encounter poorly-behaved inmates at times. You will be manipulated many times; it's just the nature of the prison culture. And if you work in a medium or higher custody level facility, it is perhaps only a matter of time until you could potentially be bodily threatened by an inmate.

Do not be surprised when some inmates are found to be well-connected to "security threat groups" both inside and outside the prisons. Ask your coworkers about STG groups.

Your pen and paper will eventually turn into written notes that end up in an infraction being issued for inmate misbehavior. The idea of holding inmates accountable for misbehavior may illustrate one of the key differences between your role as a prison facility chaplain in contrast to the religious volunteers or the part-time contracted single-religion chaplain. And though holding inmates accountable for bad behavior is a duty of all prison workers, some may seek your downfall when inmates complain to them that you have confronted the poor behavior of individuals in their niche group.

Religious volunteers are not likely to understand the need for disciplining inmates, or for being part of issuing infractions for serious misbehavior in a chapel. Prison volunteers only may see a small fraction of prison life, and may see inmates on their best behavior.

But as prison staff, use your pen and paper to note the time and facts of serious misbehavior. Do not "look the other way" from dangerous inmate behavior. Your own safety is on the line as well as that of others. Incidents of inmate misbehavior usually happen suddenly and without warning. Train yourself ahead of time so that you can respond immediately in times of need.

It is helpful to think through "what if" scenarios in your head. At the same time keep in mind that helping people to grow and change involves holding people accountable for their serious misbehavior.

Learn to have "a sharp eye, a thick skin, and a soft heart." Your intervention may save others from bodily harm. The life you save by responding to serious misbehavior of one inmate you serve may be the life of another inmate you serve. Remember where you are.

You may be part of issuing infractions when certain serious misbehaviors are carried out against yourself, or against other staff. You can know that when you take disciplinary action that is just and fair, even the incarcerated inmates you infract and who you intervene upon for their serious misbehaviors will often later acknowledge that you treated them fairly and justly.

Even such a tiny, innocuous pocket as the shirt pocket can contain tools that prevent injury, provide for public safety, and prevent loss of life. You will make a difference if you are willing to carry out this duty well.

Discussion Segment Eight Questions

1. Describe any security, investigations, or enforcement background you may have had. How might these experiences benefit your team of coworkers in the correctional setting?
2. Why should inmates be held accountable for behavior in prison?
3. As facility chaplain, what are some practical ideas for how to help religious volunteers understand why inmate accountability is important?

DISCUSSION SEGMENT NINE
Closing Reflections

This booklet explored the contents of the metaphor of a tangible, physical work "jacket." Anyone who has worn a uniform for work or for sports knows that the best uniforms are tailored to the activity. The metaphorical "Chaplain's Prison Jacket" carries practical ideas for serving today's multi-faith society by serving its prison culture professionally, with a high regard for religious literacy. The jacket is only a metaphor based on an outer garment of clothing made with many pockets.

Just and fair treatment of all inmates requires honoring the right to expression of their diverse religious backgrounds, and these pockets hold the skills to help you carry out this duty. Some of the described items are optional. The writer of this booklet does not claim to be an all-knowing expert on prison and correctional safety, security, operations, or practice. None of us know it all, and in reality the correctional, legislative, and inmate cultures are always in flux, and may vary from one correctional jurisdiction to another.

No one who works in prison religious knows everything; we just do the best we can do in the duty we are assigned.

New challenges may come along that will mirror the political and public sentiment of the outside world. Changes in demographics or legislation shape the prisons. We all face challenges and run risks as staff in today's prisons. The reality is that every day we grow and learn, and along the way we all get manipulated at times.

For long-term success inside prison culture, find coworkers who are able to act as confidants to you when inmate behavior seems to be getting the best of you in a situation. You will need a sounding board. We all need each other in this work.

Welcome to the corrections family! You will need a corrections network. And make sure that when you do make a blunder, you tell on yourself before an inmate has the chance to use your mistake against you. Most mistakes—even terribly embarrassing ones—are recoverable in this business if you honestly come clean!

Thank you for taking the time to think through what prison religious work is about. May you continue to learn and grow for a long and productive career, and through it may you bless others by a rich lifetime of lessons well-learned.

Discussion Segment Nine Questions

1. Discuss five ways this exercise has modified your awareness or understanding of the prison culture. What will you do with this information?
2. How can coworkers and prison staff members help one another inside the correctional setting?
3. What was your view of duty and calling prior to exploring prison culture? What is different now? What will you do with this new data?

SELECTED BIBLIOGRAPHY

Baysinger, Timothy G. "Right-wing Group Characteristics and Ideology," July 2006, hsaj. org/articles/166

Beckford, James A. "Social Justice and Religion in Prison: The Case of England and Wales," Social Justice Research, 1999, Vol.12 (4), 318-322

Coleman, Judith "Chaplains: God's Partners In Prison" *Corrections Today 65,* no. 7 (December 2003)

Grant, Peter, *Walls, Wire, Bars and Souls: A Chaplain Looks At Prison Life* (San Bernardino: Fynbos, 2013)

Hamm, Mark S. "Prisoner Radicalization: Assessing the Threat in U. S. Correctional Facilities," October 27, 2008, NIJ Journal No. 261, nij.gov/journals/261/pages/prisoner-radicalization.aspx

nasa.gov/audience/forstudents/k-4/dictionary/Season .html

Smith, Earl *Death Row Chaplain: Unbelievable True Stories from America's Most*

Notorious Prison (New York: Howard, 2015)

usno. navy. mil/data/docs/EarthSeasons. Php

Made in the USA
Las Vegas, NV
31 August 2023